LAW EXAM COMPANIONS:

TORT LAW

A Comprehensive System for Conquering Torts Exams

CONTENTS

HOW TO USE THIS COMPANION

This companion provides a guided framework to approach torts exams and operates as a simple, comprehensive system that reduces the anxiety of exam-taking by ensuring that no points get left behind. This companion gives law students the final tool for a successful exam by providing a way for students to quickly and effectively record the issues spotted in a fact pattern. As a result, the system ensures that no points are missed.

In the end of semester scramble to synthesize all of the information covered in a law course, students often turn to hornbooks and explainers to identify and re-learn the most important information in each class. After creating a broad outline and understanding the general twists and turns of tort law through these materials and their general class notes, students can then turn to this guide as an exam companion.

It is recommended that after creating a general outline, students find sample exam questions from their own school, online, or in commercial sources. Then, they can sit down with their outline and this companion to tackle those sample questions.

It is also encouraged that students create their own personal version of this companion's general framework. Through an iterative process of taking practice exams and then analyzing gaps in their knowledge and notes, students will be able to create a personal version of this companion specifically tailored to their class. The companion itself as a system ensures that each issue on the exam is quickly tackled, analyzed, and checked off the list.

* * *

A note on substantive material: this companion is a general framework for tort law exam taking and can only supplement and not replace any materials on the substantive law of torts, especially as it varies from jurisdiction to jurisdiction. In addition, this companion does not comprehensively cover intentional torts, rather, it is suggested that for each intentional tort covered in a course, the student create an additional, separate sheet which lists out that specific tort's elements and any relevant defenses. If the issue of an intentional tort comes up on their exam, it is advised to use that sheet so as not to forget any elements of the claim. Rather, use this framework as a high-level approach to conceptualize how to structure your exam-taking method.

STEPS TO SUCCESS

1. **Gather your materials**, including class notes, commercial guides, outlines from other students, etc.

2. **Create a general outline** of your understanding of tort law that works for you, maybe through handwritten or typed re-creation of all the material or a more simple, distilled form. Whatever your style is, have a method of information retention that allows you to double check your understanding of an issue if any come up in the study process.

3. **Review the companion** to familiarize yourself with the process and general framework.

4. **Find sample exam questions.** These can be through your school inventory, an online search, or a commercial resource. Ideally, your sample questions will also have answers that allow you to check your work.

5. **Simulate exams**. Sit down and work through these questions, using this guide and your outline as a companion. As you get closer to the exam, make your setting more realistic by simulating, as much as possible, the exam conditions including time restraints. In answering the questions, be sure to analyze both sides of the claim, specifically highlighting where the plaintiff and defendant would make differing arguments.

6. **Re-create and edit this companion** as you work through questions, to best supplement your own outline and the material you will be tested on.

7. **Have confidence** on the day of the test, knowing that you have your own personalized walkthrough to rely on that ensures you will quickly find and defeat every possible issue on the exam without missing any points.

USING THE COMPANION:

Most torts exams present the exam taker with a complicated fact pattern and ask them to tease out all possible claims and their merits. This companion is meant for those exams.

To use it, simply read the fact pattern through and decide how many potential claims there are. A "potential" claim should be read broadly, as students should assume even weak claims or those that are clearly missing elements should be analyzed, giving the student an opportunity to demonstrate their knowledge.

For example, if the fact pattern has parties Steve and Kelly, and Steve might have reason to sue Kelly, simply write *S v. K* in the "Claim" column of the Aggregator. Then, document each claim in the Aggregator by marking the issues that come up.

The various elements of a tort action are split into separate pages in the Analyzer for clarity, but for efficiency, students may choose to economize a final version to bring into their exam that lists each element without any page or section breaks.

On the Aggregator, check off and annotate anything that will need to be discussed in your answer as an issue. Document everything you will need to analyze, from whether the elements are all there to if there are potential issues of affirmative defenses, the type of liability, etc.

Then, for each claim listed on the Aggregator, create a separate Claim Analyzer sheet, labeled at the top by the suit named in the "Claim" column of the Aggregator (*S v. K*). Read the facts again and fill out that sheet, which breaks down each issue you have flagged in the Aggregator into subcategories and allows you to fill in notes or circle things that will need to be analyzed in your essay.

After creating an Analyzer for each claim, re-read the facts a final time to make sure you didn't miss anything, checking your Analyzer and Aggregator with the facts. This is a very important step, as usually fact patterns are dense, and this allows additional issues to jump out at you.

When you are satisfied that your Analyzer and Aggregator are comprehensive, you now have a small stack of Claim Analyzers that are essentially the outline of your exam answer. Just head over to your exam software or bluebook and get going on your A + answer.

One by one, go through each claim analyzer and break down each issue you have flagged. Walk through the elements, defenses, and other considerations for each claim, analyzing the strengths and weaknesses of each given the legal, practical, and policy considerations. With the companion, you shouldn't have missed any issues and should have an efficient method to turn your outline bank of Analyzers into a top-grade submission. With practice, the procedure and material will become so familiar that you can enter the room on exam day with confidence that you are going to be setting the curve.

CLAIM AGGREGATOR

	Elements						Additional Considerations							
Claim	Duty	Breach	Fact	Proximate	Damages	Emotional	Defenses	Res Ipsa	Landowner	Strict Liability	Product Liability	Joint/Several Liability	Statutory	Respondeat Superior

CLAIM ANALYZER

CLAIM: _____

DUTY:

____ **General duty** not to create an unreasonable risk of physical harm through one's conduct.

____ **Special duty** [circle:]

(common carrier; innkeeper; landowner; custody; undertaking; professional; negligent entrustment; relation with person posing risks (parent, custodian, employer, mental health); non-negligent creation of risk; social venture; misrepresentation; criminal acts; or landlord/tenant).

____ Duty of **Landowner** to (invitee, licensee, trespasser, or non-flagrant trespasser) (unless attractive nuisance).

____ Reasonable in the circumstances to **non-flagrant trespasser**;

____ reasonable care and investigation to known and unknown dangers for **invitee**;

____ warn but not eliminate for **licensee** (safe as for self); or

____ refrain from wanton or willful injury of **trespassers** (unless attractive nuisance).

____ **Emotional** liability (zone of danger; bystander; foreseeable).

____ **Vicarious** liability (respondeat; parents; joint enterprise).

____ **Products** liability (manufacture; design; warning).

____ **Strict** liability (abnormally dangerous activity; animal; product (manufacturing, retailer, express warranty).

<u>BREACH</u>:

____ Conduct fell below **objective standard** of reasonable care in the circumstances;

>____ **unless** child or physically disabled (then subjective if not adult activity or reasonable for disability) or conduct requiring specialized knowledge.

____ Conduct fell below a **higher or other standard** (common carrier, professional, landowner).

____ If **products liability** (pick: **risk** or **consumer** test):

>____ Failure to conform to own standard;

>____ unreasonable design;

>____ or inadequate warning

>>____ without learned intermediary, sophisticated user or obviousness defense.

Because:

____ Conduct was unreasonable given comprehensive judgment of **foreseeability** (includes general foreseeability, relevant custom, utility, alternatives, and BPL formula (burden less than severity * likelihood)).

____ **Statutory** breach

>____ Being a relevant type of accident and

>____ type of person and

>____ no excuse applies; then either a rebuttable presumption of breach **or** evidence of breach, where statute sets floor as minimum standard.

____ **Res Ipsa**

____ Where condition would not normally occur and

____ is within exclusive control of defendant (unless newer standard) and

____ no contributory negligence by Plaintiff;

____ then there is either an inference or presumption of negligence.

____ Landowner because failure to meet [above identified standard].

____ Professional custom (failure to meet relevant standard).

Evidence is:

____ Direct

____ Circumstantial

<u>CAUSATION</u>

____ But for (when multiple necessary **or** multiple possible causes **and** would not have happened anyway).

____ Substantial factor (when multiple sufficient causes).

____ Alternative Causes (when multiple negligent defendants create exposure and uncertainty as to which caused harm); burden shifts to defendant.

Evidence is

____ (direct, statistical, specific, other).

<u>PROXIMATE CAUSATION</u>

____ **Foreseeable** Outcome, including foreseeable:

____ **Harm** within the risk;

____ **Type** of harm;

____ **Plaintiff**;

____ **Extent** of harm (considering eggshell rule);

____ **Manner** of Harm;

____ no superseding or intervening causes.

<u>DAMAGES</u>

____ **HARM** occurred, including:

    ____ **Monetary** (costs past and future)

    ____ **non-pecuniary** (pain and suffering).

____ **Survival** Action; **Wrongful Death** Action (consortium).

____ **Joint and Several**

    ____ joint liability for single theoretically indivisible harm or

    ____ single practically indivisible harm.

<u>DEFENSES</u>

____ No Duty **or**

____ Duty negated by assumption of risk:

    ____ express;

    ____ implied;

    ____ primary.

____ **Comparative** negligence **or** secondary implied assumption of risk.

____ **Contributory** negligence and jurisdiction applies either 50% **or** 51% rule (where allowed if Plaintiff is up to or as negligent as defendant (51), **or** not as negligent as defendant (50).

___ Superseding cause per proximate analysis.

<u>**NOTES and CHECKS:**</u>

INTENTIONAL TORT

____ Intent

____ Elements of the tort (battery, assault, false imprisonment, trespass to land or chattel, conversions, intentional infliction of emotional distress) [suggested that a separate checklist is made]

____ Defenses (consent, self-defense, defense of others, necessity)

Made in the USA
Monee, IL
12 September 2024

65651997R00016